VOLUME 1

SWEAR WORD
FLORAL MANDALA

Adult Coloring Book Designs

STRESS RELIEVING PATTERNS

COLOR TEST PAGE

COLOR TEST PAGE

Fuck Off

Douche
bag

Fuck

Piece of shit

Calm Your Balls

Asshole

Bollocks

Bitch Face

Asshat

Basic bitch

Screw You

Bullshit

Bitchy

Shit

Go to Hell
Bitch!

Dickhead

Bellend

Holy Shit

Cuntface

Lameass

Fuck that Shit

Bloody hell

Assface

fuckface

Shitbag

Fanny

www.ingramcontent.com/pod-product-compliance
Lightning Source LLC
Chambersburg PA
CBHW081858280526
45789CB00007B/2747
9781539398271